Raised by Wounds
I Am the Child Who Chose to Break What Broke Us

JK Hogan

Copyright © 2025 JK Hogan

All rights reserved.

No part of this book may be reproduced, distributed, or transmitted in any form or by any means, electronic or mechanical, including photocopying, recording, or by any information storage and retrieval system, without the prior written permission of the publisher, except for brief quotations used in reviews or critical articles.

Published by Hogan House Publishing

ISBN-13 : 979-8-9942100-3-1

Printed in the United States of America

Introduction

WE DIDN'T GROW UP learning love. We grew up learning how not to make things worse.

We learned how to stay quiet, how to read moods, how to shrink ourselves in environments that were supposed to protect us. Some of us were yelled at. Some of us were ignored. Some of us were praised only when we performed. Many of us learned early that affection came with conditions.

So we adapted—not because we were weak, but because we were children.

By the time we became adults, survival had already settled into our nervous systems. It shaped how we communicate, how we attach, how we argue, how we withdraw, and how we mistake intensity for intimacy. We weren't raised by love. We were raised by wounds—and wounds don't teach you how to feel safe. They teach you how to endure.

Contents

1	1
The First Lesson Was Silence	
2	4
Do As I Say, Not As I Do	
3	7
Love Was Conditional	
4	10
Survival Mode Became a Personality	
5	13
The Five Love Languages Are Symptoms	
6	16
Why We're Drawn to Chaos	
7	19
Why Peace Feels Boring	
8	22
Reparenting the Self	
9	25
Learning Safety as an Adult	

10	28
Breaking the Inheritance	
Epilogue	31
What We Choose Now	
About The Author	34

1

The First Lesson Was Silence

BEFORE WE EVER LEARNED what love was, we learned what not to do. We learned not to talk back, not to ask too many questions, not to cry unless something was visibly wrong, and not to embarrass the adults. Above all, we learned not to make things harder.

That was the real lesson. It was never written down, but it was enforced every day through tone, punishment, withdrawal, and the way comfort was delayed, made conditional, or denied altogether. Very early on, we learned that our emotions were not something to be understood. They were something to be managed.

So we managed them. We swallowed words that needed to be spoken. We numbed feelings that needed attention. We adjusted ourselves to environments that refused to adjust to us. When we were told, "Do as I say, not as I do," we didn't hear guidance. We heard contradiction.

Children do not learn integrity from instructions. They learn it from consistency. What we were actually being taught was that authority did not require accountability, love did not require safety, and respect was something you owed rather than something you were given.

We observed anger erupt without repair. We watched affection disappear when expectations were not met. We saw adults demand emotional control while modeling none of it themselves. Somewhere along the way, we stopped asking whether something was right and started asking how to survive it. That shift changes everything.

Silence became our first language, not because we had nothing to say, but because saying it came at too high a cost. Silence protected us from being hit, shamed, or abandoned emotionally or physically. Over time, we became fluent in it. We learned to read rooms before books and moods before math. We learned to anticipate reactions instead of expressing needs.

This is often mistaken for emotional intelligence, but it is not. It is hypervigilance. Hypervigilance can look impressive on the outside and is often praised as maturity, resilience, or strength beyond one's years. Internally, it is a nervous system stuck on constant alert, scanning for danger in places that should feel safe.

That is not strength. It is adaptation, and adaptation comes at a cost.

By adulthood, survival was no longer something we did. It was something we were. It shaped how we loved, what we tolerated, and who we chose. We confused chaos with connection, inconsistency with passion, and intensity with intimacy. Peace did not feel familiar. It felt suspicious.

When a person grows up surrounded by emotional unpredictability, calm does not feel safe. It feels like the moment before something goes wrong. As a result, stable, communicative, emotionally available relationships do not create excitement. They create discomfort. The body does not relax. It waits, and that waiting becomes exhausting.

This is where love begins to fracture, not because it is unwanted, but because it was never modeled in a healthy form. Love was not demonstrated as protection, emotional safety, or presence. It was demonstrated as control, obligation, and sacrifice without boundaries.

Later, when love is explained through concepts like the five love languages, people often cling to the one that feels familiar. Not because it defines them, but because it exposes what was missing. Gifts resonate with those who were neglected. Words resonate with those who were criticized. Touch resonates with those deprived of affection. Time resonates with those who were never prioritized. Acts of service resonate with those who had to earn care.

These are not preferences. They are symptoms. They are markers of deprivation. Instead of asking why so many adults are desperate to be loved in specific ways, we normalize the hunger without examining the famine that caused it.

What was truly lost was not love itself, but safety. The safety to express emotion without punishment, to make mistakes without shame, and to exist without performing. When safety is absent in childhood, it does not automatically appear in adulthood. Many people spend years trying to build relationships that can finally provide what they never received, without realizing they are asking partners to heal wounds they did not create.

This is how resentment grows, cycles repeat, and love collapses under the weight of unspoken expectations.

Most people are not afraid of love. They are afraid of being unprotected inside it. Afraid that relaxing will cause everything to fall apart, that needing too much will lead to abandonment, or that being fully seen will result in rejection. These fears were learned, not imagined.

Until we confront what raised us—the wounds, the silence, and the survival—we will continue mistaking familiarity for fate.

This book is not about blaming parents. It is about telling the truth. Healing does not begin with forgiveness. It begins with clarity. Clarity begins when we finally say out loud what we were taught to keep quiet.

We were not raised by love. We were raised by wounds, and that distinction matters.

2
Do As I Say, Not As I Do

THIS WAS NOT JUST a phrase. It was a system. It taught authority without accountability and obedience without understanding. Adults demanded behavior they did not demonstrate and punished children for noticing the difference.

"Do as I say, not as I do" communicated several unspoken rules. Adults did not have to live by the standards they enforced. They did not have to regulate their emotions, but children did. They did not have to explain themselves, but children owed compliance. Questioning that system came at a cost, and we learned that early.

We were told to control our emotions while watching adults lose control of theirs. We were told not to yell while being yelled at, to be respectful while being disrespected, and to be honest while witnessing lies, denial, and avoidance treated as normal. An environment like that does not teach discipline. It teaches confusion.

Children are wired for coherence. They need words and actions to match. When they do not, a child does not assume the adult is wrong. The child assumes they are. Over time, that contradiction becomes internalized. Love can hurt and still be called love. Apologies become optional for those with power. Accountability flows downward but is rarely practiced upward.

Most damaging of all, children learn that their reality is negotiable. When adults say one thing and do another, children stop trusting their own perception. They begin questioning themselves instead. Maybe I misunderstood. Maybe I am too sensitive. Maybe this is normal.

That is how self-doubt is installed. Not through one defining moment, but through thousands of small dismissals. Being told what you saw did not happen. Being told how you felt was not valid. Being told your reaction was the problem rather than the behavior that caused it.

That is not discipline. It is emotional gaslighting. Gaslighting does more than confuse a person in the moment. It fractures their relationship with their own intuition.

So adaptation follows. Children learn to read people instead of trusting themselves. They anticipate moods instead of expressing needs. They stay quiet instead of staying honest. Honesty is not unsafe because it is wrong, but because it is inconvenient. In homes where truth threatens stability, integrity is not taught. Performance is.

Say the right thing. Do the expected thing. Hide the rest.

These patterns do not disappear when childhood ends. They follow people into adulthood, into friendships, workplaces, and especially intimate relationships. This is why boundaries are so difficult for many adults. Boundaries were not modeled as healthy. They were modeled as punishment, withdrawal, or control. As a result, setting them feels wrong, dramatic, or selfish.

When boundaries are crossed, self-doubt resurfaces. Am I overreacting? Am I asking for too much? Is this just how love works? These questions are not signs of weakness. They are the result of conditioning.

The "do as I say, not as I do" system also taught something quieter but equally damaging. Image mattered more than truth. Appearances were protected at all costs. Dysfunction was hidden. Conflict was buried. Pain was handled privately, if it was handled at all.

That is how cycles survive. Not because people do not know better, but because they refuse to see better.

As adults, many people recreate what they know. Some become controlling because chaos once dominated their lives. Some become emotionally unavailable because vulnerability was never safe. Others overextend themselves because love once had to be earned. Without realizing it, they repeat the same dynamics that harmed them, just in different forms.

Not because they want to, but because familiarity feels safer than the unknown.

Here is the difficult truth. Healing cannot occur in an environment that requires you to doubt yourself. Many adults are still living by internal rules written by people who never had to live with the consequences. Rules like not talking about it, not feeling too much, not challenging authority, and not trusting your instincts.

Those rules kept people compliant. They did not keep them healthy.

Breaking this pattern does not begin with confrontation. It begins with recognition. Recognizing that inconsistency was the wound. Recognizing that confusion was not your fault. Recognizing that clarity is not disrespect. Recognizing that real leadership and real love do not demand obedience without example.

Love that must be enforced was never love. It was control. Until that lesson is unlearned, dominance will continue to be mistaken for strength and compliance for peace.

The truth is simple, even if it is uncomfortable. We did not fail to follow the example. There was no example to follow. Once that is seen clearly, it becomes possible to stop living by rules that never protected you in the first place.

3

Love Was Conditional

WE DID NOT GROW up believing that love was something you received. We grew up believing it was something you earned. Love appeared when we behaved, achieved, stayed quiet, or avoided causing problems. It disappeared just as easily.

Love came with terms we were never allowed to negotiate. These were unspoken rules that shifted depending on the mood in the room, the stress of the day, or the emotional capacity of the people in charge. Children learned to be good, useful, grateful, and smaller. This was not guidance. It was conditioning.

When love is conditional, a child does not feel secure. They feel monitored. Every interaction becomes a test. Every mistake feels like a threat. Every emotional expression carries risk. In response, children learn to self-edit.

They learn which parts of themselves are acceptable and which must be hidden. Anger becomes "difficult," sadness becomes "dramatic," and fear becomes "weak." Those emotions do not disappear. They are swallowed because there is no safe space for them to exist.

Conditional love does not always look abusive. Sometimes it looks polite. Sometimes it looks functional. Sometimes it looks like a roof overhead, food on the table, and clothes on one's back, offered as proof that nothing more should be needed. But provision without presence is not love, and survival without safety is not care.

Children need more than basic needs met. They need to be emotionally held. When that does not happen, the message becomes clear even if it is never spoken aloud. Needs are too much. Feelings are inconvenient. Worth is tied to behavior.

That message follows people into adulthood. It appears in how hard they work for approval, how afraid they are to disappoint, and how quickly they abandon themselves to keep others comfortable. Over-giving, over-explaining, and overcompensating are not signs of generosity. They are signs of fear that love will be taken away.

When relationships feel uncertain, the nervous system does not settle. It activates. People chase reassurance, tolerate inconsistency, and mistake crumbs for commitment. Conditional love teaches that inconsistency is normal.

This is why rejection feels so intense. It does not only affect the present moment. It reopens the original wound and confirms a belief carried since childhood: if I am not enough, I will be left.

As a result, people tolerate what they should not, remain silent when they should speak, and shrink when they should stand firm. Losing love once felt like losing everything, so preserving it becomes the priority.

Conditional love also teaches something dangerous about power. It teaches that the one who withholds has control, that affection can be used as leverage, and that distance functions as discipline. In adulthood, people either submit to that dynamic or recreate it.

Some become over-accommodating. Others become withholding. Some chase. Others stay just out of reach. Both roles originate from the same place: a childhood where love did not feel safe.

One of the hardest truths to accept is that many people were not unloved. They were loved inconsistently. Inconsistency can be more damaging than absence because it keeps hope alive while safety remains out of reach. It teaches people to wait, to try harder, and to believe that if they get it right, love will finally stay.

That belief does not fade with age. It deepens.

This is why unconditional love feels unfamiliar. When someone offers steadiness, suspicion arises. When communication is clear, hidden meaning is searched for. When someone remains present through difficulty, the body braces for withdrawal.

Conditional love trains people to expect disappearance. Instead of resting in connection, they monitor it, manage it, and prepare for its loss. That is not intimacy. It is emotional labor rooted in fear.

Healing does not require casting caregivers as villains. It requires honesty about what was missing. Love without consistency is not safe. Love without emotional availability is not secure. Love without accountability is not stable. Love that disappears when someone is human is not love. It is approval.

If you were raised on conditional love, you did not fail at relationships. You were trained for them. Trained to perform, tolerate, and confuse anxiety with attachment.

Unlearning that pattern takes time. It requires awareness and the courage to believe that love is not something you earn by disappearing. Real love does not test or threaten. It does not keep score.

It stays.

4

Survival Mode Became a Personality

AT SOME POINT, SURVIVAL stopped being a response and started becoming identity. Not because it was chosen, but because it worked. It kept people safe, needed, and invisible when visibility carried risk. Over time, it became automatic.

No one wakes up and decides to be hyper-independent, emotionally guarded, overly responsible, or constantly alert. These traits form in environments where relying on others is unreliable and vulnerability is unprotected. Survival strategies develop quietly, shaped by necessity rather than intention.

People learn to do things on their own, stay ready, and function without support. These adaptations are often praised. That is where the trap begins. Survival behaviors are frequently mistaken for strengths. Hyper-independence is labeled confidence. Emotional detachment is called maturity. Overworking is rewarded as ambition. People-pleasing is framed as kindness.

What looks impressive on the outside is often exhaustion on the inside. Survival mode is not sustainable. It is reactive, always bracing for impact. When it becomes a personality, rest starts to feel unsafe.

In survival mode, the nervous system never fully powers down. There is constant scanning, anticipating, and preparing for something to go wrong. Even in calm moments, the body remains tense. Even in healthy relationships, the mind stays alert. Relaxation does not come naturally. Waiting does. Over time, waiting becomes the baseline.

This is why joy feels brief, peace feels unfamiliar, and stillness feels uncomfortable. In the past, stillness often preceded something bad. The body remembers that association long after the danger has passed.

Survival mode also shapes how people relate to others. Many become the fixer, the caretaker, the dependable one, or the strong one. Not because they want to, but because being needed once felt safer than being loved. If others relied on them, abandonment felt less likely. If they held everything together, things would not fall apart. If they needed little, disappointment could be avoided.

As a result, people minimize themselves. They stop asking for help, expressing needs, and trusting that support will arrive consistently. Independence, once empowering, slowly becomes isolating.

This is where relationships begin to strain. Survival mode does not know how to receive. It only knows how to manage. People give more than they get, tolerate more than they should, and stay longer than is healthy. When genuine support is finally offered, it feels unfamiliar, uncomfortable, and undeserved.

Often, that support is pushed away or tested. A part of the nervous system is still waiting for the moment it disappears.

Survival mode also creates contradiction in intimacy. People crave closeness but pull away when it arrives. They want to be seen but hide when attention turns toward them. They desire intimacy but feel exposed inside it. This is not dysfunction. It is protection. Protection that once preserved safety but now limits connection.

Survival mode keeps a person alive, but it does not allow them to live. It prioritizes control over connection, predictability over presence, and self-sufficiency over intimacy. As long as someone operates from it, love feels like work because relationships become something to manage rather than something to experience.

Letting go of survival mode can feel terrifying. Not because it is harmful, but because it is familiar. It was the strategy, the armor, and the way through.

Putting it down can feel like exposure, weakness, or stepping into danger without protection.

But survival mode is no longer protection. It has become a cage. Cages do not always look like pain. Sometimes they look like competence, control, and composure.

Healing does not require erasing who someone became. It requires recognizing that who they became was a response, not their essence. No one is born hyper-vigilant, guarded, or exhausted. These traits are learned. What adapts can change.

The goal is not to stop being strong. It is to stop needing strength just to feel safe. The life being built does not require survival skills. It requires presence. Presence becomes possible when the nervous system learns something new: the danger has passed.

5

THE FIVE LOVE LANGUAGES ARE SYMPTOMS

THE FIVE LOVE LANGUAGES did not emerge because love was finally understood. They emerged because many people were trying to make sense of why love never felt complete. In response, love was categorized and compartmentalized in an attempt to explain what was missing.

Receiving gifts, quality time, words of affirmation, physical touch, and acts of service were not discoveries about love itself. They were translations. They provided language for what was absent during formative years, when it mattered most.

Love was never meant to function in isolated parts. A clean home is not defined by washing dishes alone. A meal is not complete because it includes protein. Health is not measured by a single vital sign. When something is whole, its elements work together. Love functions the same way.

Healthy love is integrated. It includes presence, care, protection, consistency, affection, communication, and accountability operating together. When those elements exist, no single expression has to carry the weight of safety.

When adults feel dependent on one specific expression to feel loved, it is not preference. It is information. It signals unmet needs that trace backward rather than forward.

People do not crave gifts because they are materialistic. They crave them because effort was absent. People do not crave words of affirmation because they are insecure. They crave them because criticism outweighed encouragement. People do not crave physical touch because they are needy. They crave it because affection was withheld. People do not crave quality time because they are demanding. They crave it because they were never prioritized. People do not crave acts of service because they are controlling. They crave them because care once had to be proven.

These patterns are not personality traits. They are adaptations.

The issue is not the concept of love languages. The issue arises when symptoms are mistaken for identity. People begin to say, "This is just how I'm wired," or "This is my love style," and treat unmet needs as fixed traits. Without realizing it, unmet childhood needs are transformed into adult demands.

When that happens, responsibility for healing is placed on partners who did not create the wound. That dynamic is neither fair nor sustainable.

This is where relationships begin to strain. Two wounded people end up negotiating survival strategies instead of building connection. One partner needs constant reassurance while the other feels overwhelmed. One expresses love through action while the other feels unseen without words. Instead of asking what is underneath the conflict, arguments focus on expression. Delivery is debated while origin is ignored.

Love languages can be useful when they help people identify needs. They become harmful when they replace self-awareness. When someone claims a love language without examining why it feels necessary, growth stalls. Patterns repeat while expectations remain unmet.

Healing does not occur when someone finally expresses love in exactly the right way. Healing occurs when a person understands why that expression feels necessary for emotional safety.

The difficult truth is that no single person can compensate for what was missing in childhood. No amount of gifts, words, time, touch, or service can undo years of emotional deprivation if the wound itself remains unacknowledged.

That does not mean relationships are hopeless. It means honesty is required.

Healthy love does not feel like hunger. It does not feel like waiting, proving, or convincing someone to show up in one specific way in order to feel secure. Healthy love feels consistent, predictable, and safe.

Safety is what many people were searching for all along.

The five love languages did not fail. They revealed the truth. Many people were raised with fragments of love rather than an integrated whole. As adults, they attempt to assemble wholeness from those fragments without ever having experienced what wholeness feels like.

This chapter is not about abandoning the concept of love languages. It is about refusing to stop there. When the wound heals, the symptom quiets. When safety is established, expression becomes flexible. When security is present, love no longer needs to prove itself.

6

Why We're Drawn to Chaos

THIS PATTERN IS NOT accidental. People do not repeatedly end up in chaos by chance. They recognize it. The body locks onto it before the mind has time to evaluate. Before logic, before standards, and before red flags can register, familiarity pulls attention toward instability.

Chaos feels like home.

When early experiences of love involved instability, emotional swings, silence, criticism, or fear, the nervous system learned a central rule: connection equals tension. As a result, tension later registers as intimacy. Raised voices feel like passion. Hot-and-cold behavior feels like desire. Uncertainty feels like depth. Calm, by contrast, feels suspicious.

There is an uncomfortable truth beneath this attraction. Chaos creates a sense of importance. Unpredictability demands attention. It keeps people engaged, analyzing, adjusting, and trying harder. For those who had to earn love early in life, effort becomes synonymous with meaning.

In stable, mutual, and emotionally clear relationships, there is nothing to chase. There is no role to perform, no task to complete, and no emotional puzzle to solve. There is only presence. Presence can feel terrifying when safety was never established early on.

Chaos also keeps people occupied so they do not have to feel. Constant reaction prevents reflection. Managing someone else's emotions distracts from sitting with one's own. When a relationship is unstable, full trust is never required.

In this way, chaos protects against vulnerability. Vulnerability requires safety, and safety requires the nervous system to stop bracing.

This dynamic is often mislabeled as chemistry. What many people call chemistry is nervous system activation. The rush, pull, fixation, and difficulty disengaging are not signs of love forming. They are signs of survival wiring being triggered. The body does not differentiate between healthy and unhealthy familiarity. It only recognizes what it knows.

This explains why red flags often feel intriguing rather than alarming. Emotional distance, unavailability, and inconsistency do not feel foreign to someone raised in emotional unpredictability. They feel recognizable. As a result, they are explained away, romanticized, or reframed as depth, complexity, or misunderstanding.

In reality, this is often an attempt to resolve unfinished emotional patterns by recreating familiar conditions and hoping for a different outcome.

There is another function chaos serves. It provides an excuse not to choose. As long as a relationship remains unstable, full commitment can be postponed. Real attachment does not have to be risked. If the relationship collapses, chaos becomes the explanation rather than fear.

Peace can feel boring because boredom is what occurs when the nervous system is no longer in crisis. For those whose baseline was constant alert, peace can feel like deprivation. It can feel as though something is missing or that something bad is about to happen.

In response, stimulation is often manufactured. Arguments are initiated. Doubt is introduced. Distance is created. This is rarely conscious. It is instinctive. Then it is rationalized with statements like needing excitement, not having met the right person, or wanting something more intense.

What is often being expressed instead is discomfort with safety.

It is important to be clear. Chaos is not passion. Intensity is not intimacy. Anxiety is not attraction. These are trauma responses mistaken for romance. As long as they remain confused, people will continue choosing relationships that reinforce familiar wounds, regardless of how self-aware they believe themselves to be.

Healing does not begin when someone stops being drawn to chaos. It begins when they become honest about why the attraction exists. When familiarity is acknowledged as unsafe. When excitement is recognized as erosive rather than nourishing. When something that looks like love is named as costly to peace.

That honesty marks the beginning of change.

When safety is experienced long enough for the nervous system to recognize it, chaos loses its appeal. It stops feeling magnetic and begins to feel loud, repetitive, and empty.

At that point, the work shifts. The challenge is no longer finding love, but learning how to remain present when nothing is escalating and nothing is on fire.

7

Why Peace Feels Boring

PEACE DOESN'T FEEL BORING because it lacks depth. It feels boring because your nervous system was never trained to live without threat.

When chaos was the background noise of your childhood, calm doesn't register as safety. It registers as absence. There's no urgency, no problem to solve, no emotional signal to track. As a result, the body stays alert, waiting for something to happen.

Peace doesn't activate survival skills. It doesn't require hyper-awareness or emotional management, and it doesn't give you a role to perform. If your sense of worth was built on being useful, strong, or needed, peace can feel like irrelevance. When there's nothing to fix, you're left asking who you are without the role.

For people raised in instability, boredom isn't empty. It's threatening. Boredom creates stillness, and stillness creates awareness. Awareness brings feelings that were once unsafe to feel, including grief, anger, fear, and loneliness.

Chaos kept those emotions buried. Peace gives them space. That's why the nervous system resists it.

This is why stable relationships can feel "off." There's no chase, no emotional guessing, and no spike-and-drop cycle to keep adrenaline flowing. Communication is clear, affection is consistent, and conflict doesn't escalate. Instead of relief, restlessness shows up.

People begin searching for flaws, creating distance, or questioning attraction, not because something is wrong, but because the body hasn't learned how to rest yet.

Peace also removes distraction. In chaos, attention is always external, responding and managing outcomes. In peace, there's nothing to hide behind. There's no drama to justify anxiety and no instability to explain exhaustion. What remains is the self and whatever was never fully processed.

This is where many people sabotage healthy connections. They start arguments, pull away emotionally, choose someone more "exciting," or convince themselves something is missing. But what's missing isn't passion. It's familiarity.

Peace feels boring when the nervous system equates excitement with danger and danger with connection.

Here's the difficult truth: peace requires presence. Presence requires vulnerability, and vulnerability requires safety. Safety was never guaranteed growing up, so peace can feel like exposure rather than comfort.

People don't leave peaceful relationships because they don't care. They leave because peace asks them to stay fully present, without armor, distractions, or survival roles to hide behind. That level of presence feels threatening when love once meant bracing for impact.

What most people don't realize is that peace doesn't stay boring. Boredom is a transitional phase that occurs when the nervous system is no longer overstimulated but hasn't yet learned how to enjoy calm.

Over time, peace becomes grounding, then steady, then deeply nourishing. But that shift only happens if you stay long enough for the body to learn that nothing bad is coming.

Peace doesn't remove intensity. It redirects it toward growth instead of defense, connection instead of control, and depth instead of drama. That transformation can't happen if you leave the moment things get quiet.

This chapter isn't asking you to settle. It's asking you to tell the difference between safety and boredom, calm and emptiness, peace and lack. Once the nervous system relearns what safety feels like, peace stops feeling boring.

It starts feeling like home.

8

Reparenting the Self

At some point, awareness stops being enough. A person can understand their trauma, name their patterns, and trace reactions back to their origins and still continue repeating them. Insight alone does not heal wounds. Experience does.

If safety, consistency, and emotional regulation were not taught in childhood, they do not arrive automatically in adulthood. No one comes later to install them. That responsibility transfers.

Reparenting the self does not mean blaming yourself for what happened. It means refusing to let what happened continue deciding how you live. It means becoming the steady presence you needed when no one else was capable of providing it. Not perfectly, but consistently.

A common mistake is trying to reparent through force. Telling yourself to get over it, be stronger, or stop reacting is not reparenting. It is repetition. Neglect cannot be healed with neglect. Control cannot be healed with control. Shame cannot be healed by shaming yourself for still carrying wounds.

Reparenting begins with protection. Protection takes the form of boundaries, not walls or punishment, but clear limits that define what is safe, acceptable, and yours to carry. For someone who grew up without protection, saying no can feel aggressive. It is not. It is corrective. You are not being difficult. You are being responsible.

Reparenting also requires consistency. Not intensity or grand gestures, but reliability. Showing up for yourself when it is uncomfortable. Choosing what is steady over what is familiar. Maintaining routines that calm the nervous system instead of chasing what activates it.

This stage often feels boring. That boredom is not failure. It is rewiring.

A reparented self learns emotional regulation not by suppressing feelings, but by staying present with them. Emotions rise and fall without destroying you. Discomfort does not require escape. You learn that it is possible to feel deeply without reacting destructively. This is what safety actually feels like.

Reparenting also involves learning to self-soothe without self-abandonment. This is not numbing, dissociating, or overworking. Healthy soothing teaches the body that presence is reliable. You are here. You are not leaving. Care does not have to be earned through performance.

Most people were never taught this. They learned distraction instead.

As this work deepens, relationships begin to change. When you stop asking others to regulate your nervous system, you stop choosing people who benefit from your dysregulation. You chase less, over-give less, and confuse intensity with connection less. This does not happen because you stop wanting love, but because you no longer need another person to make you feel safe inside your own body.

Reparenting the self does not make a person cold. It makes them grounded. You still feel deeply, still care, and still connect. What changes is that emotional survival is no longer handed over to someone else.

The process is quiet. There is no dramatic breakthrough and no overnight transformation. There are only repeated choices that do not look impressive to anyone else but gradually change everything. Choosing rest instead of chaos, honesty instead of appeasement, and safety instead of familiarity, again and again.

The goal of reparenting is not independence. It is secure dependence. The ability to lean without collapsing, to love without losing yourself, and to remain present without bracing for impact.

That is what should have been learned early. If it was not, it can still be learned now.

Reparenting is not about fixing yourself. It is about finally giving yourself what you were always worthy of: protection, consistency, care, and safety. Not someday. Now.

9
Learning Safety as an Adult

SAFETY IS NOT SOMETHING a person can think their way into. It cannot be affirmed, manifested, or reasoned into existence. Safety is learned through experience, repetition, and often discomfort. When safety was missing in childhood, encountering it in adulthood feels foreign, not because it is wrong, but because the body does not recognize it yet.

Adult safety looks very different from childhood safety. No one steps in to rescue you. No one regulates the room for you. No one guarantees consistency. Safety becomes a choice that must be made repeatedly.

This is where many people struggle. They say they want safety but continue choosing stimulation. They say they want peace but remain engaged with chaos. They say they want stability but resist the discomfort of calm. Safety requires something most people were never taught: staying.

Staying does not mean tolerating harm. It means tolerating neutrality. Quiet evenings, predictable communication, and emotional steadiness often unsettle a nervous system conditioned by instability. The body reacts not because something is wrong, but because it is unfamiliar with being okay.

In these moments, instincts begin to misfire. Thoughts arise suggesting something is missing, something is off, or something should feel more intense. These signals are not intuition. They are conditioning.

Learning safety requires new reference points. Attention shifts from internal narratives to bodily responses. After interactions, the question becomes whether the body feels regulated or depleted, settled or tense, seen or managed. Safety leaves the nervous system calmer than it found it. Chaos leaves it activated. That distinction matters more than attraction ever will.

Adult safety also involves tolerating disappointment without collapse. Safe people will still frustrate you, misunderstand you, and fail at times. The difference is repair. Repair is what safety looks like in real time. There is no disappearing, no punishment, and no emotional withdrawal. There is accountability and return.

This is where self-sabotage often occurs. Many people mistake conflict for danger and discomfort for threat. They leave at the first sign of imperfection because imperfection once led to harm. Safety does not require perfection. It requires repair, and repair requires staying present through discomfort.

Learning safety also means developing discernment. Not everyone deserves access. Not everyone is unsafe, and not everyone familiar is healthy. Safety requires selection. You do not owe closeness to people who destabilize you. You do not owe explanations to those who repeatedly violate boundaries. You do not owe loyalty to environments that demand self-abandonment. This is not avoidance. It is maturity.

Safety also involves allowing yourself to be seen. This is not performative vulnerability or emotional dumping. It is real visibility. Letting people see you without editing for approval. Allowing relationships to develop without rushing intensity or chasing reassurance. At first, this feels exposed because control is being replaced by trust in process.

There is a truth few people are prepared for. Learning safety as an adult can be lonely. People are outgrown. Expectations shift. Others may feel disappointed or confused. This does not mean something has gone wrong. It often means chaos has lost access, and chaos tends to react when peace is chosen.

Over time, the nervous system begins to settle. Reactions soften. Choices become clearer. The question shifts from whether something excites you to whether it supports regulation.

Safety does not shrink life. It makes life livable. It creates the conditions for joy, intimacy, creativity, and depth. None of those thrive under constant threat.

Learning safety as an adult does not eliminate fear. It teaches that fear does not have to control behavior. Once safety is known in the body, not just understood intellectually, the compulsion to chase what hurts diminishes. Pain is no longer required to feel alive.

10

Breaking the Inheritance

Trauma does not disappear on its own. When it is left unaddressed, it remains active in reactions, relationship patterns, and definitions of what feels normal. It shows up in what people tolerate, repeat, and pass down without naming.

Inheritance is rarely intentional. More often, it is unfinished. When nothing interrupts it, it continues.

Breaking the inheritance does not require perfection. It requires awareness. Awareness of what is carried forward, what is tolerated, and what is modeled in everyday behavior.

Healing is not a private process when other people are involved. Regulation is felt in relationships, just as dysregulation is. Children absorb what is normalized around them. Partners learn what love looks like through consistent behavior rather than stated intention. Responsibility exists whether or not it is acknowledged.

This is where accountability replaces blame.

No one chooses their wounds, but responsibility begins with what is done with them. Ignoring wounds does not create strength, and understanding them alone does not complete healing. Awareness without behavioral change simply delays repetition.

Cycles are broken through consistent action rather than insight alone. That action is rarely dramatic or visible. It is quiet, repetitive, and often uncomfortable.

Breaking the inheritance looks like pausing instead of reacting, repairing instead of withdrawing, listening instead of controlling, and choosing safety over familiarity even when familiarity feels easier. These changes do not announce themselves, but they compound over time.

Many people stop at awareness. They learn the language of healing without altering their behavior. They explain their actions rather than correcting them. Explanation can provide clarity, but it does not create transformation.

When children are involved, this work becomes essential. Children do not need perfect caregivers. They need regulated adults who repair mistakes, apologize when necessary, and manage their own emotions rather than transferring that burden to a child. That shift alone interrupts generational patterns.

When children are not involved, the work still matters. Legacy is not limited to bloodlines. It exists in influence, leadership, and presence. It exists in how others feel after interacting with you.

Pain is either examined or passed forward. There is no neutral outcome.

Breaking the inheritance also requires grief. Grief allows acknowledgement of what was missing without minimizing it or reframing deprivation as strength. Without closure, wounds continue seeking resolution through relationships that were never meant to carry that weight.

Healing does not erase the past. It alters the future by changing behavior in the present. History remains intact, but repetition does not have to continue.

You were raised by wounds, and that was not your fault. What happens next is a choice.

How you love, how you regulate emotion, how you respond under stress, and how you remain present during discomfort all shape what is passed forward.

Breaking the inheritance does not eliminate struggle. It prevents struggle from being unconsciously transferred.

This is no longer a story centered on survival. It becomes a story shaped by agency. The cycle is interrupted when safety is chosen over familiarity, presence over protection, and truth over silence.

That shift begins with awareness, continues with responsibility, and ends with deliberate action.

Epilogue
What We Choose Now

IF YOU HAVE MADE it this far, it is because something in this book reflected a pattern you recognized. Not specific events or details, but a way of relating, reacting, and surviving that felt familiar.

That recognition is not accidental. It signals readiness.

There comes a point after awareness where avoidance is no longer possible. The realization settles that no one is coming to undo what happened. Parents cannot rewrite the past. Partners cannot compensate for childhood wounds. Time alone does not resolve unresolved patterns.

That realization can feel heavy, but it can also be freeing. When no one else is responsible for repairing the past, no one else controls what happens next.

Healing rarely announces itself. It shows up quietly in smaller reactions, longer pauses, and a reduced need to explain yourself to people who are unwilling to understand. It shows up when rest is chosen without guilt, when intensity is no longer chased, and when environments that require self-erasure are left behind.

Change becomes visible in behavior rather than declaration.

Many of us grieve the childhood we did not receive. That grief matters. Loss does not disappear simply because survival occurred. Acknowledging what was missing allows mourning to complete what denial prolongs.

While the past cannot be reclaimed, the present offers something different. It offers choice.

Choice in how relationships are entered, how boundaries are held, how emotions are regulated, and how safety is prioritized. Choice in whether familiarity continues to dictate decisions or whether awareness reshapes them.

Healing does not eliminate difficulty. Life remains complex, demanding, and uncertain. What changes is the internal relationship to that difficulty. Struggle no longer requires self-betrayal. Pain no longer needs to be recreated to feel real.

Breaking cycles does not look heroic. It looks uneventful to those still living inside chaos. It may feel uncomfortable to people invested in denial or threatened by your regulation.

That discomfort does not require correction.

There will be moments when familiar patterns attempt to reassert themselves. Old dynamics will feel tempting. Intensity may momentarily appear easier than steadiness. Those moments do not indicate failure. They indicate habit.

Each time safety is chosen anyway, the nervous system learns something new.

Rest does not have to be earned. Presence does not require performance. Love does not require suffering to be legitimate.

You were raised by wounds, but you are not obligated to pass them forward.

You can be the interruption. Not through perfection, but through consistency. Not through control, but through presence.

Over time, something subtle shifts. The body settles more quickly. Decisions become clearer. Relationships feel less effortful.

Life does not become painless, but it becomes less combative.

This book does not mark the end of healing. It marks the end of silence around it. And that shift creates the conditions where change can actually take root.

About The Author

JK Hogan was born and raised in Chicago, where early exposure to different people, stories, and realities shaped the way he listens and sees the world. He earned a B.A. in Rhetoric from DePaul University, studying how language, storytelling, and attention shape belief, identity, and human behavior.

At the same time, JK spent years serving as a youth pastor, working closely with people navigating faith, pain, doubt, and transition. That combination of formal education and lived, relational experience grounded his ability to listen deeply and speak honestly—without abstraction or distance.

In 2013, JK moved to Dallas, Texas, continuing a life shaped by travel, observation, and meaningful conversation across cultures and environments. His writing reflects that path: thoughtful, direct, and rooted in real experience rather than theory.

For inquiries or correspondence:
raisedbywounds@jk-hogan.com

www.ingramcontent.com/pod-product-compliance
Lightning Source LLC
Chambersburg PA
CBHW010330030426
42337CB00026B/4887